"...His grace toward me was not in vain..."
1 Corinthians 15:10

KISS THE SHAME OF YOUR PAST GOODBYE

LATRÉCIA C. FRIESON

UNAOPOLGETIC Copyright © 2020 All rights reserved.

The unauthorized reproduction or distribution of this copyrighted work is illegal. No part of this book may be reproduced or transmitted in any form or by any means, including electronic or mechanical means, including photocopying, recording, or by any information storage and retrieval systems, without express permission from the author. The only exception is in the case of brief quotations for reviews.

Usage Copyright Information

The Holy Bible, New King James Version®. Copyright © 1982 by Thomas Nelson, Inc. All rights reserved. Scripture taken from the New King James Version. Copyright © 1982 by Thomas Nelson, Inc. Used by permission. All rights reserved.

COVER AND INTERIOR DESIGN: RMGRAPHX

ISBN 978-1-7336503-7-3

Contents

Day One: A Personal Reflection — 1
   Looking in the Mirror… — 3
   In Sickness and In Health — 7

Day Two: But by Grace… — 23
   The Past — 25
   NOT IN VAIN. — 30

Day Three: I am what I am — 39
   I AM WHAT I AM — 41
   It is Time to Get Comfortable With You! — 43

Day Four: This is Me — 55
   It's all about Grace — 57
   The Totality of You — 59

Day Five: Do the Work — 73
   Do the Work — 75
   No One Can Out Do You, Boo! — 79
   Living Unapologetically — 91

About the Author — 95

Foreword

Here is a devotional book that is so desperately needed in our world. This is not a book about being perfect. Neither is this a book that champions the humanistic ideal of boasting in one's efforts, in the hopes to convince you that you are more qualified over someone else. On the contrary, if you have ever teetered between the blessed assurance of graciously being approved by God and yet haunted by the events of your past that clamor for all to know that you are not worthy to do what you are called to do, then this book is for you!

LaTrecia C. Frieson uses powerful truths, largely based on the writings of the Apostle Paul, that will empower you to boldly stand in the grace of God alone. What makes this message so impactful is that it is saturated in the truth that God alone is the qualifier and the One who gives His approval and commissioning to unworthy people, and through His grace we are what He sees us to be.

Is the author being extreme when she postulates that the believer can live unapologetically in the grace of God or is she on to something that, quite frankly, has been underutilized and undercommunicated in the body of Christ? Paul testifies that our Lord Jesus said, "My grace is sufficient for you, for My strength is made perfect in weakness." (2 Cor. 12:9, NKJV).

I agree with Elder Frieson concerning this relevant and timely message. I agree with others who have ever struggled to live boldly in the new identity that Christ brings to all of those who have been saved by faith and through grace alone. It takes God's amazing grace to move us towards a new day of progress and you will be blessed as you learn how to live unapologetically.

Leonard Frieson, Jr.
Senior Pastor & Founder
Generation of Praise Christian Church

A Note from the Author

Thank you for your purchase! It is my prayer that this five-day devotional helps you on your journey to live out the richly rewarding life Christ has purposed for you. This devotional is the first of a three-part devotional series, I've called UNBOXING. Too many of us live confined in the boxes we have designed for ourselves or ones imposed on us by others. Today is your day to GET OUT OF THE BOX!

To start, let's get UNAPOLOGETIC. Once we catch our stride on this topic, we can move on to becoming UNMADE and UNASHAMED! For now, we will just take one step at a time.

Let's Make a Few Things Clear…

First, let us define what UNAPOLOGETIC is not and what it is.

What it is not…

Living by God's unapologetic grace toward us does not grant us a license for an unrepentant heart or deeds. Living by God's unapologetic grace does not mean we never seek forgiveness or offer it.

What it is…

For the purposes of this devotional, being unapologetic is simply understanding that despite our downfalls and shortcomings, through the Lord's unmerited favor and abiding love we can live out our lives through His grace without shame or fear. We must own what we have done without apologizing for who we are.

Our goal…

It is my hope that like the Apostle Paul, we will begin to shift our focus away from the things we think disqualify us from living in the grace of God's love and steady ourselves in the work He has given us to do.

And do it…UNAPOLOGETICALLY.

Selah.

kissing shame goodbye

Day One: A Personal Reflection

I will praise You, for I am fearfully and
wonderfully made;
Marvelous are Your works,
And that my soul knows very well.
~Psalm 139:14 NKJV~

Looking in the Mirror...

I am going to start off real personal—real fast.

Psalm 139 is an all-time favorite bible verse of mine for so many reasons. Growing up, I struggled with many insecurities—primarily my outward appearance. Like many teenage girls I admired supermodels and celebrities and did whatever I could to keep up with whatever was trending. Lord knows whatever color Mary J. Blige dyed her hair I eagerly followed suit!

Still, my biggest challenge was I always thought I was overweight. I suppose being curvy and short seemed odd to me when I young and I did whatever I could to keep my weight at what I considered an "acceptable level."

Not even my closest family and friends knew I struggled with moderate bulimia or how I would often rush to the restroom after eating just to keep even a half of a cookie out of my system. I rarely ate at lunch—save a snack here or there. It was pretty rough.

My primary outlet was dance and I pushed myself hard. Starting dance classes at a young age, was the only place where I felt incredibly good about myself because it was based on my talent alone. Not my looks. Unfortunately, that all came crashing down when one visiting dance instructor told me how my height and curves would make me an unlikely candidate to go any further than the community circuit.

His words crushed me, and I quit dancing that day.

Oh how I wish I had the strength of Misty Copeland at that age!

With my family stretched in multiple directions at the time, my quitting did not draw any major attention and became just another thing off the to-do list. And just like that, my pain was able to go undetected.

Or so I thought.

Without dance there seemed to be such a major hole in my life, and I wasn't really sure what to do with all my extra time.

Now enter boys.

Like most girls my age that didn't seem to be too odd. It was the thing to do, right? Except what I most wanted from teen boys was to affirm my appearance. If I was accepted, I was happy—but when I wasn't, I was devastated. While I was able to hide behind an outwardly strong demeanor, I continued to shrink inside.

During that time, I allowed my insecurities to rob me of real connections with people because I so desperately wanted them to affirm something in me that could only be done through the power of God's grace and love.

And while my family did a great job telling me I was beautiful; I didn't believe them. I figured they were only saying what I wanted to hear—or at least what they were supposed to say because they were family. Thankfully, during that time my family and I maintained our church attendance.

I am glad we did.

One Sunday changed it all for me.

My pastor was teaching on the Psalms and Psalm 139 came up. Although his subject at the time only revolved around verses seven through twelve, I kept reading through verse fourteen. As he shared how there was no where we could go from the presence of God, my eyes were fixed to the fourteenth verse.

I had never seen this verse before.

Something changed in me that day.

The thought of being "fearfully and wonderfully made" struck a chord deep within me! Never had such a notion entered my mind. As I continued reading the Psalmist declare, "Marvelous are Your works and that my soul knows very well," I felt a change take over me. I realized I had never thought of God's act of creating me as a marvelous work or something that I knew about very well.

With all the topics of not sinning, the ten commandments, obedience, and forgiving others somewhere the topic of God's act of creating me as a marvelous work got lost. Perhaps I just wasn't listening—or missed church that Sunday.

Yeah, let's go with that.

The good thing is I know it now.

Meditating on that scripture and others like it enabled me to grow beyond a dependency on my outward appearance and turn toward a thankfulness to God for knowing that I am fearfully and wonderfully made despite of any trending norms or celebrity standards.

I AM A MARVELOUS WORK!

It is a scripture that many of the women at my church have heard from me on more than one occasion. When I became a pastor's wife, I made it my goal to speak words that declare how much of a "marvelous work" the women in my church are. Anytime I've heard them speak even a hint of a disparaging word about themselves, it is a word I purposely sow into their hearing.

I want to do for other women what I needed when I did not think of myself as marvelous work.

And for many years I kept that scripture close to my heart, but I do not think I knew I would still need it in my adulthood even more than my teen years.

In Sickness and In Health

Sure, I was far from my bulimic days or seeing myself through a distorted mirror image, but it only took a traumatic life event to almost revert me into my old ways of thinking. This event was so shattering that I was doubtful that either Psalm 139:14 or the unconditional love of my best friend and husband would be enough to keep me tethered to the truth of God's word.

In 2009 after several visits in and out of the hospital, seizures, and heart complications among other things I was diagnosed with Lupus. Between the issues with my heart and seizures the doctors were doubtful I would survive.

Things got so serious I was effectively told to write my will.

Thankfully, it was not God's plan for my life to end that day.

Through prayer and the support of my husband, family, and friends I proudly boast that I am a Lupus Survivor!

But that survival came at a cost.

The doctor put me on steroids to aid my ongoing complications and health challenges. I had seen what steroids did to others and I was not happy about it, but I realized it was the least of my worries.

Or so I thought.

Between my immobility due to Lupus and the weight I gained on the steroids, I eventually gained more weight than I ever did with three pregnancies. Not only did I feel my insecurities creep back into the corners of my mind, like the Serpent in the

Garden, I fell for the bait like Eve and listened.

Psalm 139:14 now seemed like nothing more than a nice thing to know, but not something I actively practiced. How could I be a "marvelous work?" To me, I seemed like anything but.

My husband was only three years into his pastorate and his visibility in the Kingdom was growing. He had preaching engagements left and right and I hated more than anything for him to be seen with me.

Not only had I gained weight, but with the immobility I had lost the only thing that I loved, dancing and movement. I was so uncomfortable with myself that I felt like people saw my weight before they saw me.

You see, years after I was first delivered from my teen insecurities, I looked back at pictures of myself and realized I was never as heavy as I thought. As a matter of fact, I realized I was a tad delusional. I was like, "Girl you were cute!" God even made a way for me to dance again in my late teens and early adulthood. My pastor allowed me to start the first dance ministry at our church and I taught dance there for almost ten years before my husband was sent to pastor his own church.

Until Lupus I only lived just beyond the

shadow of my insecurities. I had no idea how close the shadows were coming to eclipse the light of God's truth. In truth, my insecurities were brewing under the surface.

Throughout the first few years with Lupus I went through bouts of acceptance and insecurity. Some good days. Some bad. Now, I knew better than to relapse into bulimia—I now had three little lives looking to me to not engage in such behavior. Besides, as an ordained minister I knew entertaining even the idea was both morally and biblically wrong.

But what about my thought life? Well that was all on me. Or so I thought.

Ultimately, I discovered what we bury in our minds or our hearts will ultimately come out of our mouth. That is exactly what I needed. I needed to hear just how badly I spoke about myself with my own ears so that the minister in me could finally confront that foolishness.

Often when I'd run into people I had not seen in a while I would be sure to tell them I had succumb to Lupus and have been on steroids. Somewhere in the darkly insecure corners of my mind it was my way of justifying my weight gain and perhaps elicit some a measure of empathy.

Then one day it happened.

I heard the Holy Spirit say to me, ***"Why are you apologizing for living?"***

My how that hit me hard!

> **STOP APOLOGIZING FOR LIVING!**

I was in effect, apologizing for living. I could not believe it.

Sure my immobility and steroids may have contributed to my weight gain, but did that mean I was no longer a "marvelous work?" Of course not. In fact, it was the furthest thing from the truth.

The truth is I owe no one an explanation for my appearance. The truth is I only owe the Lord my gratitude, not a passive attitude about my current state. The truth is Psalm 139:14 is just as effective for the teen who hid under the shadow of her insecurity as it is for the woman who now used it like a blanket to cover herself like fig leaves in the Garden.

The truth is that just like Adam and Eve: I was never naked.

At that moment I confessed my insecurities to the Lord and repented of replacing the truth of His word with my fears. I allowed the Holy Spirit to remind me that my self-worth was not tied to how I looked on the outside. I acknowledged that my self-worth is not tethered to any work I have done or could ever do.

Why is all of this so important?

Because we can never truly live an unapologetic life without first looking in the mirror. How can we ever expect others to respect our unapologetic stance if we are still bound by our own boxes of insecure thinking, self-condemnation, and a lack of trusting God?

Living unapologetically requires us to fully accept and trust God's design for our lives. I had to learn to trust that even in my perceived nakedness I was in fact covered by the truth of God's Word. If we do not adequately deal with our own reflections, we will quickly sink in the hole of the judgement of others.

We must learn to rejoice in who God has created us to be and trust His plan for our lives. Just as God knew one day, I would face Lupus; He also knew that through Him I am more than a conqueror.

Perhaps your inner battle is not your outward appearance or a health crisis. It could be your finances, career, or family situation. God doesn't want you apologizing for living for fear of how others think. Maybe you are the person in your family who "made it." God doesn't want you to shrink in order to make others comfortable. Your life situations don't require the comfortability of others in order for you to live the life God has for you.

You just have to live it!

Unapologetic Declaration: I AM PRAISEWORTHY!

Let us reexamine Psalm 139 in the New Living Translation:

Thank you for making me so wonderfully complex!
Your workmanship is marvelous—how well I know it.
~Psalm 139:14 NLT~

DAILY CONFESSIONS

- Thank You, Lord for the wonderfully complex creation of—ME! Despite what I consider my shortcomings, it is indeed wonderful!

- Thank You, Lord for the meticulous care you took to create me! Now when I look in the mirror of my life, I will admire just how marvelous it is!

- Lord, help me to dedicate more time appreciating this life you gave me and less time focusing on what I do not like.

My Prayer:

Lord enable me to stop apologizing for my self-regarded shortcomings and live in the unapologetic grace of Your truth.

But by the grace of God I am what I am, and His grace toward me was not in vain; but I labored more abundantly than they all, yet not I, but the grace of God which was with me
~ 1 Corinthians 15:10 NKJV~

Day Two: But by Grace...

But by the grace of God ...
~ 1 Corinthians 15:10 NKJV~

The Past

Now that we have dealt with our pesky reflection in the mirror, it is time we get that rearview mirror in check too! While we may not spend our days glaring in our rearview as much as we do our forward-facing window, this vantage point is equally important.

Any decent driver knows that you must keep a watch for what is coming up from behind or you might find yourself in an accident or worse. However, good drivers also know they cannot keep their eyes glued to their rear or they would put themselves and others in danger.

Nonetheless, it is vitally important to keep a balanced view of your surroundings. Keep your gaze set before you while being keenly aware of things around you.

Now that we have taken a deeper look at our insecurities, we must consider our past.

The truth about the past is simply this: *WE ALL HAVE ONE.*

We are all an *ex*-something.

One of the basic Roman's Road teachings reminds us, "There is none righteous, no, not one" (Romans 3:10 NKJV). The chapter even goes on to judiciously declare that "All have sinned and fall short of the glory of God" (Romans 3:23). You've heard this before, right? It is a sobering reminder, so we don't get too haughty or think we actually deserve the Lord's gracious gift of salvation.

On the surface it might seem like an easy truth to comprehend. But what if your past seemed to you so vile, so disgusting, so ludicrously inhumane that it appeared unimaginable for God to use you?

This is where we find the Apostle Paul today.

Before his conversion experience on the road to Damascus, the Apostle Paul went to extreme measures to discredit the Early Church by casting them in prison and pronouncing their deaths. Paul vehemently despised the Early Church and considered them blasphemous and in direct contradiction with both the current Jewish order and its religious teachings. Simply put, he saw them as enemies to Yahweh.

As enemies of God, Paul believed himself vindicated to pursue the imprisonment and execution of anyone who called Jesus the Messiah. In his self-proclaimed righteousness he honestly thought he was doing God a service.

Then came his Damascus Road experience. The Bible tells us Paul was still "breathing out threats and murder against the disciples of the Lord," (Acts 9:1) when he began his journey to Damascus. That is, until Jesus came. After a bright and blinding light that threw him from his high horse, Paul said,

> Who are You, Lord? Then the Lord said, "**I AM JESUS**, whom you are persecuting"
> ~Acts 9:5 NKJV~

Isn't that just like Jesus, knocking us off our high horses just when we think we are big and bad?

Once Jesus revealed Himself to Paul his life changed.

Forever.

The Lord sent a disciple named Ananias to go to Paul and assure him of

Our work is to proclaim JESUS IS LORD!

his encounter with the Lord and he later baptized him. However, when Paul began to preach in the synagogues in Damascus that Jesus was Lord many said, "Is this not he who destroyed those who called on this name in Jerusalem, and has come here for that purpose, so that he might bring them bound to the chief priests?" (Acts 9:21).

Rightfully, people feared Paul. After all, wasn't he the same man who consented to the stoning death of the Stephen (Acts 7:59 & 8:1) and who was known to make "havoc of the church?" (Acts 8:3) Why should the disciples believe the sincerity of his alleged conversion? How many loved ones had died under Paul's vile contempt? How many families had been torn apart?

There were so many reasons not to either accept or believe his testimony that he had in fact seen the Risen Christ.

However, the truth is simply this: neither their acceptance nor belief in his testimony changes the truth of it.

The truth is that the Lord had revealed Himself to Paul. The truth is Paul repented. The truth is Paul accepted Christ and was baptized. And with his newly found belief in Christ, Paul had as much right as any Believer to boldly proclaim Jesus as the

Risen Lord!

Too often, we allow the opinions of others to stunt our forward growth and movement in Christ. I suppose because so many people "remember us when" it can easily cut short our progress if we let it.

Can you imagine what would have happened if Paul sulked in the shame of his past? What if Paul never wrote his many letters to the Churches of Ephesus, Philippi, Corinth, and countless others?

Who then would have admonished a young Timothy to fight the good fight and let no one despise his young age? Would someone else see to the care of Onesimus to Philemon so that together they would continue sharing their faith? Even more, who would have given Titus the qualities of a sound Church and the standards by which Elders should be weighed?

Sure, God in His sovereignty could have raised someone else to take on such a momentous task; but that was not His plan.

No. This was all God's plan for Paul's life.

Just as Paul had an assignment to the Church, so do each of us. We are all here to make a difference. Whether big or small, word or deed; every Believer has a responsibility to labor in the continual work of the Kingdom of God.

And that work is to proclaim JESUS IS LORD !

It is for this reason we cannot allow the shame of our past to hold us hostage from the effectual work of the Kingdom. Like Paul, we must endeavor to proclaim the Gospel of Christ and do so UNASHAMED (we will talk about that some more in the next devotional).

NOT IN VAIN.

Is My Living in Vain is one of my favorite songs from the iconic gospel group, The Clark Sisters. I imagine Paul would echo the heartfelt sentiments of the lyrics of this song passionately. Paul declared in 1 Corinthians 15:10 that God's grace toward him was not in vain. He believed that despite his past wrongdoings and the gnawing shame of such a past, God still lavished His divine grace upon his life.

While our past sin and its shame is continually in our rearview, we must not allow it to condemn us or block us from the future that awaits us in Christ. God's grace on our life is not some colossal mistake. No. It is the unmerited favor of the Father's precious love toward us to encourage us to know that no matter how shameful our past, His grace is no blunder or misgiving.

In fact, God's grace is intentional.

God's grace is governed by His unwavering love for His children. It is God's steadfast love toward us by which Paul declares in Romans 5:8 "But God demonstrates His own love toward us, in that while we were still sinners, Christ died for us."

The intentionality of God's grace is so powerful and pure that even before our personal Damascus experience, Christ died for our sins. His grace did not wait for us to be perfect. So why would we let our imperfections prevent us from serving Him with our all?

Unapologetic Declaration: KISS SHAME GOODBYE!

So let us work through our past. Together.

Taking another look at the middle of part of 1 Corinthians 15:10, what does Paul explicitly state about God's grace?

"…His grace toward me was not in vain"

Now, take time to think of your most egregious sin and errors. Below fill in the blank and allow today's confessions to help heal the wounds of your past hurts and shame.

DAILY CONFESSION

- Your grace **is not** wasted on me despite the time I _____
- Your grace **is sufficient** to cover every vile thought and deed.
- Your grace **is not** contingent upon my righteousness or good works.
- **Your grace covers both my past and future**.

My Prayer:

Lord, I lift my past to You. As David declared in Psalms 51: 3-4, "For I acknowledge my transgression, and my sin is always before me. Against You, You only, have I sinned," but I thank You for Your Grace. Your grace for me is not vanity. I will no longer fret over my rearview mirror and past shame. Instead, I ask to boldly walk in the abundance of your grace for me.
In Jesus Name. Amen.

_____
_____
_____
_____
_____
_____
_____
_____
_____
_____
_____
_____
_____
_____
_____

Day Three: I am what I am

"But by the grace of God, I am what I am…"
~ 1 Corinthians 15:10 NKJV ~

I AM WHAT I AM

I AM WHAT I AM

Ever heard the phrase, "take me as I am or leave me alone" or "take it or leave it?" Aside from the obvious negative connotations, this is often a stance we must take in living in the grace of an unapologetic life.

Why you may ask?

Because even for the best of us we all are pressing toward the mark, as Paul declared, which is the upward calling through Christ Jesus. Despite being the colossal apostle himself, even Paul stated that he had "not apprehended" such a prize—or hit the mark. He was pressing; as we all are in Christ.

None of us can claim to have arrived. At best we can proclaim we are on our way. As we all are being transformed from glory to glory.

Too often we stunt our own growth in our walk with Christ because we focus on our shortcomings or on the parts about ourselves, we wish we could change. We even let the criticism of others that we "aren't qualified enough," to stop us short of pursuing what God has called us to do in the Kingdom and in the world.

Instead of giving in to feelings of inadequacy we should simply state, I am what I am.

One of the first steps in truly becoming unapologetic is to own what we have done without apologizing for who we are. Being unapologetic does not mean we do not have things to repent of, but it doesn't mean we should walk around with a woeful spirit.

There is enough pressure from the world, our employment, social media, family, and friends to go around. The last thing you need is to be your own worst enemy. If Paul continually harped on his past heinous deeds, I doubt he would have been such a catalyst for the Church as we know it today.

Even more so, it makes it harder for God to use someone who is so focused on all that they are not that they fail to see all God has created them to become. As a matter of fact Paul even declared that we are continually being transformed "from glory to glory." (2 Corinthians 3:18)

How will we ever see that glory revealed if we give up on who we are?

It is Time to Get Comfortable With You!

One of the reasons we get bogged down by the opinions of others and the insecure thoughts we have about ourselves is because we have yet to get comfortable with the person we see in the mirror.

Instead, we often see ourselves:
Through societal trends
Through the experiences of our past
Through the eyes of our family
Through our financial status
Through our education
Through the opinions of others
Through our past hurts and pain

We need to learn to embrace our flaws, our quirks, our past, our status without letting those things alone define who we are in Christ. Sure, these things may influence our lives, but they do not have to be the summation of our existence.

Thinking back on when I needed to come to terms with being a "marvelous work" through Christ I had to first learn how to embrace the woman I saw in the mirror. Flaws and all. I recall standing bare before my mirror and thanking God for everything I saw as an imperfection. I thanked Him for the round tummy that helped bring three beautiful humans into the world. I thanked Him for the scars that only symbolized I survived. I thanked Him for it all!

I had to learn to get comfortable with my own nakedness.

Most of us do not take time to examine who we are apart from the coverings we use to hide who we really are. Too often, we can't wait to throw a towel on our bodies after we bathe because we are not accustomed to being comfortable with our bare selves. Fully uncovered.

Much like Adam and Eve, we reach for the first fig leaf we can find because we feel ashamed and exposed.

This feeling doesn't just apply to physical nakedness. Rather, it applies to any area where we feel naked or exposed. We do not take enough time getting comfortable with who we are; so it is no wonder we are not pressing toward the goal like we should.

At some point we must accept who we are, past shame and present sins included. Even for the strongest of us, we too often live under the guise of what we consider our strengths while cautiously sweeping our struggles under the rug. Instead of dealing with our past hurts and pain, we toss the feelings of our tormented emotions aside. We do so hopeful we do not have to do the unpleasant work with how that hurt exposed our nakedness.

I imagine Paul felt unworthy to declare the Gospel of Christ as the shadow of his past loomed around him.

In 1 Corinthians 15:9, the Apostle Paul says, "For I am the least of the apostles, who am not worthy to be called an apostle, because I persecuted the church of God."

Thankfully, he did not allow the egregious nature of his past to prohibit his newly unapologetic stance as he stood flat-footed and preached the Gospel to both Jews and Gentiles alike. He acknowledges that he doesn't consider himself worthy, but he chooses not to let his own self analysis of his worth to determine his ability to serve in the Kingdom of

God.

At some point, we must fully accept God's forgiveness of our sins. We must daily remind ourselves that God is fully aware of who we are when He chooses us to His work. He isn't caught off guard by our pet peeves or our quirks. He is well-informed of things that cause us to stumble and stray. And yet, He still calls us to serve in fellowship with Him.

I am often comforted by the gracious words of Romans 5:8, which says, "But God demonstrates His own love toward us, in that while we were still sinners, Christ died for us." The finished work of the Cross is just that—a FINISHED WORK! God is not waiting for me to do anything different before He calls me unto Himself. As a matter of fact, even Paul (Saul) was still on his persecution campaign when God called him in mid-stride.

Accept who you are TODAY!

So many of us are waiting to "get our act together" before we begin doing the work of Christ. Unfortunately, Romans 3:10 also reminds us "There is none righteous, no, not one." Some of us are waiting for an imaginary bloom of perfection to hang a halo over our heads before we make a move in the work of the Kingdom. Rather, why not accept who you are today and begin moving in His grace?

Let's be clear, we cannot ask others to "take us as we are" if we haven't truly accepted who we are through Christ.

That said, this is not an entirely "new testament" mindset. Throughout the Bible, and particularly the Old Testament, we can find God constantly correcting self-defeating mindsets. Not only did God admonish Moses for thinking negatively of his speech impediment, but the Prophet Jeremiah also admitted, "But the Lord said to me: Do not say, I am a youth, For you shall go to all to whom I send you. And whatever I command you, you shall speak." (Jeremiah 1:7 NKJV)

It does not matter whether you are worried about your age, race, gender, finances, or whatever you render a shortcoming, God is not worried about it. In fact, He called you to Himself fully aware of all that you are—and it is that thing He wants to use for his glory!

Unapologetic Declaration: I AM WHAT I AM

Take a moment to look in the mirror (or use your phone—I know you have it handy). Now say to yourself: YEP I DID IT!

YEP, I DID IT

Whatever IT is, the fact is YOU DID IT! But the truth is, God knows and has forgiven you. As a matter of fact, the redemptive work of Christ on Calvary's cross is powerful enough to cover you from not only your past, but both your present and future faults.

Interestingly, God has a knack for calling some of the greatest biblical heroes at times when their lives did not seem heroic. Even the great Moses stuttered and was a murderer. Yet, and still God chose to use him for His glory. There are many others I could name like David, Noah, Sarah, Apostle Peter, and even King Solomon.

God wants to use your past, all that you are right now, and all that He plans for you to be for His glory!

DAILY CONFESSION:

- I am not perfect.
- But I am being perfected.
- I am not who you think I should be.
- But I am who God says I am.
- As Paul said, **"But by the grace of God, I am what I am."** **(1 Corinthians 15:10).**

Day Four: This is Me

"and His grace toward me…"
1 Corinthians 15:10 NKJV

It's all about Grace

Grace. It is unmerited. It is personal.

Often, when I think of God's grace, I think of it in its larger context of salvation. Recently, however, I have taken a more personal approach to understanding God's grace. While yes, it is through Christ's shed blood on Calvary's cross that God's grace and salvation is made available to all, we need to get more granular.

Very granular indeed.

Why? Because in order to account for every sin that could ever be committed by any human to ever live, God had to not only cover the collective sin of all but the singular sin of one.

I have often heard it said that if there was only one human on the earth, The Father still would not deviate from His plan of salvation. However, in order for His gift of salvation to be available for all, He had to account for every sin.

My sin is not your sin. Your sin is not necessarily my sin. Yet, collectively, God's grace is enough to cover your sin and my own.

Why is this so important to understand?

Because one can not freely become unapologetic without first understanding how God's grace is specifically and personally designed for the totality of who you are—which includes your past, present, and future state.

Living by Christ's unapologetic grace is personal.

One reason I believe God's grace is personal is because He desires a personal relationship with us. If grace was only offered as some collective bundle deal that expired or only covered sins A through D and people born on odd days, we might have a problem. Thankfully, this is not the case!

Our Heavenly Father has accounted for our every quirk, pet peeve, indifference, shortcoming, pitfall, and predicament. Understanding how personal God's grace is helps us take our eyes off all the things the enemy uses to distract and discourage our forward progress in the Kingdom of God. The enemy's goal is to keep our eyes on our flaws and failures so much that we eventually give up.

However, Paul reminds us in **1 Corinthians 15:10**, "and His grace toward me was not in vain." Despite his past atrocities toward the Body of Christ and the Lord Himself, Paul chose not to live in the dark hole of his past. Instead, he owned what he did without allowing it to stunt all he was and would eventually become. He embraced the truth. God's grace was not in vain.

And there is still no vanity found in the abundance of God's grace.

The Totality of You

You are unique. You are the only you we will ever have. There will never be another you.

Ever.

Accepting the totality of all you are both now and in the future is paramount for living out an unapologetic life. This means taking stock of everything that makes up your personhood and owning it like only you can.

Sure, it is nice to look up to others and perhaps where applicable, follow their walk in Christ. I mean even Paul said, "Imitate me, just as I also imitate Christ." (1 Corinthians 11:1) But he did not mean so at the abandonment of your own identity in Christ. Too often we come so dangerously close to idolizing our current array of personalities in the Kingdom that we try to emulate them. While there is nothing wrong with admiring our leaders in the faith, we must be careful that we don't deify them or, rather view ourselves through mirrors of comparison.

That is not what Paul meant by imitating those who follow Christ.

Instead, why not begin to accept the wonderfulness that is you!

If you are like me, you have made peace with the hard fact you will likely never be a size two or the shape of a Coke bottle. That, my friend, is quite all right. I am now intimately at peace with my curves and frame. Whether others are or not is not my battle. Nor should it be my focus or concern.

Does that mean I shouldn't do what I can to keep and maintain a healthy life? Of course not! Romans 6:1 admonishes us not to "continue in sin that grace may abound." I refuse to take advantage of God's grace toward me by reckless living. Rather, I honor His precious gift of Grace and work daily to take care of my physical, spiritual, and mental well-being.

Now ask yourself, what about you makes you uniquely you? What is it that you bring to the table that can't be offered by anyone else? Let me help you answer this—IT'S YOU! You are the gift! You are the wonderfully imperfect, perfected person the world never knew it needed until your grand arrival on your day of birth!

And we thank the Lord for YOU!

God designed a specific grace just for you! The grace He prescribed for your life is enough to cover everything you have been, you are, or will ever become. His grace covers your flaws, faults, and your failures. His grace extends to every facet of your life, including your family, job, health, and finances. That is why when the Lord told Paul "My grace is sufficient for you," (2 Corinthians 12:9) we have no need to fear that one day God will run out of grace. For every thorn among the roses of your life, God has grace enough to cover you!

It is for this reason we can truly live out an unapologetic life. Not because we have no need of repentance, but because for everything we can ever think wrong with us, God has grace to cover it. Knowing this, why should or would we walk around with a woeful or sorrowful spirit when we know that God's grace toward us is exceptionally unapologetic!

Unapologetic Declaration:

THIS IS ME!

God's specific, intentional, and personal grace toward us inspires us to live unapologetically for Him! If the Lord Himself, who is well aware of every miniscule detail of our lives thought it not robbery to extend not only His gift of salvation, but the abundance of His grace toward us, who are we not to live the fearlessly unapologetic life He designed for us?
To live a bold and unapologetic life bears no credit to our own merit, but it is justified and authenticated by His grace!

Take a few moments to meditate on each correlating scripture and recite each declaration out loud.

2 Corinthians 3:18

But we all, with unveiled face, beholding as in a mirror the glory of the Lord, are being transformed into the same image from glory to glory, just as by the Spirit of the Lord

This is me. Imperfect but being perfected. No longer am I trying to be something that I'm not. Instead, daily, I recognize I am being transformed from "glory to glory" in the likeness of Christ

_____
_____
_____
_____
_____
_____
_____
_____
_____
_____

Lamentations 3:22-23
Through the Lord's mercies we are not consumed, Because His compassions fail not. They are new every morning; Great is Your faithfulness.

This is me. A person who daily stands in need of the unending and sufficient grace of God. I am thankful that "His compassions fail not and that His mercies are new every morning".

_____
_____
_____
_____
_____
_____
_____
_____
_____
_____
_____
_____
_____

Ephesians 1:6-8
To the praise of the glory of His grace, by which He made us accepted in the Beloved. In Him we have redemption through His blood, the forgiveness of sins, according to the riches of His grace which He made to abound toward us in all wisdom and prudence

This is me. Accepted in the Beloved. I have redemption through His blood. I am forgiven of my sins and the richness of His grace abounds to me.

Day Five: Do the Work

"but I labored more abundantly than they all"
1 Corinthians 15:10 NKJV

Do the Work

Are you feeling a little better about yourself now? Good. Now it's time to get to work. If you are already working, let this be an encouragement to you to press on!

It is not enough to get our self-esteem boosted in a confident unapologetic stance if we never do the work required of us in the Kingdom of God. Make no mistake about it, God has something for you to do.

Too often we get caught up trying to do the things that are seemingly more favorable or raise our eligibility to be noticed. When in fact, God simply wants us to DO THE WORK! Whether others see us or pat us on the back for our service is purely inconsequential.

Jesus instructs us in Luke 7:9-10 not to look for thanks when we are doing the work we are commanded to do. Alternatively, the Lord explains that we should say, "We are unprofitable servants. We have done what was our duty to do."

That's right! We are unapologetic unprofitable servants.

I like that!

As unapologetic unprofitable servants we should strive to labor in the work of the Lord.

Your work in the Kingdom may not look like your friend's work. Your pastor's work may not look like his bishop's work. And guess what? That is quite all right. We are all still unprofitable servants doing only what is our duty to do.

In these interesting latter days, I believe we need to work harder in the Kingdom than ever before. However Christ leads us to work is just as personal as the grace He extends from one person to another.

When my husband first became a senior pastor, I initially struggled with what I would look like as a leading lady. Was I supposed to wear a big church lady hat? Lord knows I did not want to. Should I strive to become a copastor? It seemed like the "in thing" to do at the time but I didn't feel a calling from God to do so.

For the first few years I struggled with what being a "first lady" looked like. There were so many influences and voices telling me what to do, and even more so what not to do, that I was confused. Often, I was frustrated because I felt there were expectations looming over me that either didn't fit my personality or seemed too lofty. At the time, none of my friends were pastor's wives so while most were encouraging, it was hard for them to relate.

Praying often, I sought the Lord and asked Him to help me define what to make of this new role. As I sought Him, I was reminded of 1 Corinthians 15:10 in my quiet time. Continuing to pray, He whispered two powerful words, "BE YOU!"

No two words have gripped my heart and released my angst and trepidation like those precious words.

It was about the third to fourth year of my husband's pastoral ministry when I finally began to find my stride. Small strides, but strides just the same. Having recently been diagnosed with Lupus, I looked to the Lord to help me make priority what He wanted to be priority. One thing I learned early with Lupus was that stress was a major trigger and I did not need the stress of the expectations of others or my own to put my health in jeopardy. At the time I still suffered with severe bouts of seizures and some debilitating sensory awareness—the last thing I needed was to compound the issues with trying to be a text-book version of a first lady.

I simply needed to be me!

Our children were still young at that time, so I knew being a godly mother was paramount. Not to mention my husband and I had only been married for six years when he became a senior pastor, so it was important I held our marriage in highest esteem.

Using the Lord's prompting to be me, I knew prioritizing my home was my first ministry. That was the work I had been called to do. Just below my personal relationship with God, my family, specifically my husband and children, were where my focus belonged. Sure, I still lead our women's ministry and assisted my husband as an elder in our church, but for me, my family was where the Lord wanted me to give my energy.

Over the years not much has changed. However, now that my children are older, I have found more time to branch out into other desires of my heart.

Does this mean you can't be a wife and mother and have it all? Of course not! But what does having it all look like to you? What has the Lord prompted your heart's desire? For me, having it all meant both my marriage and motherhood were at the top of my pyramid. For you it could be another matter.

Doing the work the Lord has for you is just that—for you! Sure, your pastors and governing leaders should affirm that work in you by the leading of the Holy Spirit, but it is God's desire to use you to do that work—not some carbon copy of someone else!

No One Can Out Do You, Boo!

When Paul says he "labored more abundantly than they all," it is not a prideful or arrogant stance. Rather, I believe Paul understood when you operate in God's Kingdom assignment for you and you alone, no one can out do you!

Paul was secure in his kingdom call and he was unapologetically unashamed. In Romans 1:16 Paul declared, "For I am not ashamed of the gospel of Christ." The Apostle felt a holy obligation to both the Greek and non-Greek and to the wise and unwise to share the Gospel of Jesus Christ (Romans 1:14).

Despite many of his peers not seeing an initial need to sow God's Word to non-Jews, Paul knew that it was his task to do so.

And he did so—unapologetically.

He did so when the Jews feared him. He did so when the Greeks were intimidated by him. He did so in chains. He did so in prison.

He just did it.

Just as we must remember that God's grace is personal, we also must understand His plan—and the work He has for you to do is also personal. While there may be a corporate gathering and like mindedness of the work we do in the Kingdom, the work assigned to each believer is specifically designed for that believer.

Whether you are the lead singer or serve as a background vocalist—your work in the Kingdom of God matters! Whether you serve as an usher or in the pulpit, your work matters! There is a specificity of grace measured to you that is only at work when you work! It is a part of God's anointing on your life.

Perhaps the Lord has gifted you in administration (1 Corinthians 12:28). For some people who do administrative tasks it might just seem like filing and data entry—but for someone anointed in administration it means ensuring the efficiency, efficacy, and effectual work of the ministry in which you serve. A person anointed in administration carries a manner of excellence, knowing the devil may be in the details but has no desire to let him have his way—not on their watch!

When we do the work God has called us to do it's quite all right to say, "I labored more abundantly than they all," because like Paul you also know the latter, "yet not I, but the grace of God which was with me." (I Corinthians 15:10) The second reason Paul felt confident in the work he did in the Kingdom is because he knew God was with him!

How amazing is that!

Knowing God is with us should give us an assurance we can't find anywhere! Why? Because we are talking about the God of the Universe! The God of all creation! The God who made Heaven and Earth thinks it not robbery to be with us as we perform His good work in the earth! That, my friends is nothing short of amazing! If you ever wanted to brag on something—brag on that!

BELIEVE

Unapologetic Declaration: I BELIEVE I AM READY TO WORK!

Are you ready to do the unapologetic work God has for you? Or are you asking yourself, what is this work? If so, that's okay. Don't feel bad if you don't know in this moment the specific work God has for you to do. As a matter of fact, the Lord Jesus answered the same question from the multitudes when they pondered the same thing in John 6:28-29,

"Then they asked him, what must we do to do the works God requires? Jesus answered, 'The work of God is this: to believe in the one he has sent.'"

Do you believe in the one God sent? Do you believe in Jesus as your personal Lord and Savior?

If you answered yes, then know that is the beginning of the work. Believing that Jesus lived, died for your sins, and on the third day arose from the grave is your start to doing His work. Why? Because you can not do His work with an unbelieving and unrepentant heart.

Yikes! Did I say—unrepentant? YES! Being unapologetic is NOT being unrepentant. As a refresher from our opening, we still need to acknowledge our sin, but we live in the grace of God's unapologetic love toward us. We kiss our shame farewell because He died for us on the cross and no longer need to carry that shame. We live unapologetically for Him by doing the work He has for us and that work starts and ends with our belief in Him.

At every turn, your belief in Christ will be challenged, but you must stand firm in your convictions. It is for this reason your belief in who the Son of God is to you lays your foundation for every move you make in the Kingdom of God. Still, being human we are often faced with areas where our unbelief takes us hostage. In those moments we must cry out like the desperate father in Mark 9:24, "Lord, I believe, help my unbelief!"

Pray this with me:

Father, in the Name of Jesus I pray that you to help me to believe you in the areas where fear and doubt threaten to take over. Lord, help my unbelief. I know you have called me to do a work for you, but my unbelief is hindering me. Help me to know you are bigger than my fears. Holy Spirit, remind me you are with me. Lord Jesus, I surrender the parts of me I reserved for myself. Be Lord of my life. My whole life. My thoughts, my ambitions, my desires—my everything.

In You alone, oh Lord, I put my trust.

In Jesus Name, I pray. Amen .

NO EXCUSES
NO APOLOGIES

Living Unapologetically

Now it's time for you to live out the unapologetic life Christ has designed just for you! Use the next few pages to meditate further on the scriptures we discussed and either write out your prayers or major points and how they impact your forward growth in living unapologetically in the Kingdom of God.

_____
_____
_____
_____
_____
_____
_____

1 Corinthians 15:10

But by the grace of God I am what I am, and His grace toward me was not in vain; but I labored more abundantly than they all, yet not I, but the grace of God which was with me

About the Author

Elder LaTrecia C. Frieson is the Leading Lady of the Generation of Praise Christian Church where she serves devotedly alongside her husband Pastor Leonard Frieson, Jr. She is an anointed minister of the Gospel with an exceptional heart for women, children, and families in the Body of Christ. Much like Esther, Elder Frieson holds fast to Word of the Lord that He has placed her in the Kingdom, "for such a time as this" (Esther 4:14)

Elder Frieson graduated from the University of Maryland College Park in May 2000 where she obtained her Bachelor of Science in Family Studies. She has spent her professional career in Records and Information Management and is employed as a senior subject matter expert for a national non-profit. In May 2006 she was licensed to preach the Gospel and later ordained to the professional Christian Ministry June 2010 by Pastor Leonard Frieson, Jr., and the Generation of Praise Christian Church. Currently, she leads the women's ministry, "Women at the Throne" and is the Elder of Worship Services at GOPCC in addition to supporting her husband as Business Liaison for church affairs.

In addition to her roles in her church and professional life, she is also an Amazon Best Selling author. Under the name L.C. Son, she writes in the epic fantasy and romance genres. Her first novel, Beautiful Nightmare (Book One) was released in 2019. She has published two other full-length novels and three short stories in the Beautiful Nightmare series.

While she is a gifted speaker and teacher, her greatest

gifts are her husband and their beautiful children, Lenny, LaNaiah, and Liron with whom she loves passionately with all of her heart! Her desire is to reach the lost, restore the brokenhearted, and redeem the time through the Power of the Word of God and the anointing of the Holy Spirit!

For more information about her ministry with her husband visit WWW.GENERATIONOFPRAISE.ORG

For more information about her literary and fiction works visit: WWW.LCSONBOOKS.COM

Coming Soon...

THE COMPLETE UNBOXING DEVOTIONAL SERIES

UNMADE- Planned 2021
UNASHAMED- Planned 2022

www.ingramcontent.com/pod-product-compliance
Lightning Source LLC
Chambersburg PA
CBHW040509110526
44587CB00044B/4092